CW01667125

Mairi Murphy

Observance

To Tony,
Enjoy!
Mairi
xx.

CLOCHODERICK

Observance was first published in 2018
by Clochoderick Press.
First Edition.
www.clochoderickpress.co.uk

Cover Design by R.K. Wallace

Clochoderick Press
27 Newton Street
Paisley
Renfrewshire
Scotland
PA1 2RN

A CIP catalogue record for this book is available from the British Library.

ISBN: 978-1-912345-05-2

Typeset by R.K. Wallace in Dante 11pt

Printed and bound by:
Imprint Academic
Seychelles Farm, Upton Pyne, Exeter, Devon EX5 5HY

Funded by:
PAISLEY 2021
FOR UK CITY OF CULTURE

About the Author

Mairi Murphy lives and writes in Paisley in the west coast of Scotland. She has completed a Masters Degree, with distinction, in Creative Writing from Glasgow University. Poems from this collection can be found in the following publications: *From Glasgow to Saturn (10th Anniversary Edition) 2016, Walk in My Shoes (Read Raw Press 2012), Shetland Create (Mangold Press 2016), Underbridge Poetry 2017, From Glasgow to Saturn (10th Anniversary Edition, Issue 38, 2016), Glasgow Women Poets (Four-em Press 2016), New Writing Scotland 30 (2012), New Writing Scotland 35 (2017), Laldy! (2016, Pilot Issue).*

'CSI Madrid' and 'Memo' won first place for The Alistair Buchan Prize 2016, Glasgow University.

'Your Version' was shortlisted for The Alistair Buchan Prize, 2016, Glasgow University.

Notes on Poems:
'Annis' was inspired by and based on a character from Paul Kingsnorth, 'The

Contents

Ritual

Longing

Dreaming

Escape

Judgement

Loss

To My Dad.

Grateful thanks to the Creative Writing staff of Glasgow University for their unfailing support and encouragement, and to Mairghread McLundie (Four-em Press) whose help, enthusiasm and hard work has been invaluable.

Observance

RITUAL

Shark

loner, you don't even
click with your own species
through updraughts & canyons
I am caught in the drag
of your s-shaped heart
stir the bottom of the sea

swim in a language that doesn't know me
see with eyes that don't see me
you can break me - whole

silent I hear
the opposite of creation
the opposite of infinity
the nanosecond
of the nanosecond
before

in air bubbles you turn me inside out
a killing kindness
you breathe me through and through
incapable of filtering you can only obey
sheer instinct
constantly arguing with yourself
no you are not

on the edge of awareness
a toe in the water, waiting
I leave the ability to walk on water
sink with ordinary guilt
wear no cautionary life jacket.

In Bed with Paul Durcan

He opens up tame, periodically, like the moon
with his late flowering of love and impish turn
of phrase, as we lie in bed together,
share a toilet with five other women,
talk of wounds,
how we got them,
when they came.

We are strangers, yet all friends together,
the slipped gastric band, not fit for purpose, surely
an abscess, recently drained, an absence, you might say
though me & Clare, we share a gallbladder, or in fact did
till plucked out, without ceremony, cast adrift
swimming in formaldehyde & glued back together.

But Paul, he's the calm one giving out,
seeing absurdity in pain,
above it all
without the aid of anaesthetic
dispensing wit and wisdom
from the mountains of Mayo
at the turn of each page.

Alice Notley Reads at Stanza

Tiny anger hits the ground so hard
it splits the continent

tells me everything she is not
a shark in the shallows, yes she is

sooking in chaos like love you don't want
a two-edged sword sifting

between soul and spirit
cleaving the beating heart of you

her little life as the earth pulses
detects malfunctioning displays of harmony

she thinks succeeding is a hoax
sings in a voice I don't own.

Cloistered

He took me here
the view wasn't his to give
I wanted it
rounded pillars
fitting the small of my back
remember
soft smooth stone
shadowed deep and warm
expecting me
to stay.

Glasgow sunsets
golden
over West End windows
weeping decor &
sky-craned reflections.

Above the Clyde
floating ships
wait for a flood
tide to turn.
In Regent Moray Street
she hopes I'll go
tells me
to own the view myself
stop counting
crow stepped gables take what's mine
move on.

Smallness of Rain

I can hear volume
sounding out the unfamiliarity
of the familiar

tracing the familiarity
of the unfamiliar
the sound an absence makes

losing my perspective
in the smallness of rain
I hide

in scattered patterns of rain
everything is alternative
everything is displaced

can you be missing
the absence of sound
when hands lift off each other

smallness of rain accentuates
the sound of volume
fills familiarity with unfamiliar

alternative rain is the absence of sound
the sound an absence makes
when you are missing

Life in all its Fullness

The long line of you stretches away
unimaginative bricks bothering me
if I let them – cracked white paint
out of control, like me, like you
too much of a good thing, unrestricted
growth and red leaves, white lilac
smothered, bramble-cluttered, thorn-driven.

I could hack and hack at you.
I could shape. Prune is an awkward word,
testament to going away, form of
absence, scratch-free windows.
There should be a summerhouse on stones
still unflattened, the Japanese maple
from the Kyle of Lochalsh, Virginia creeper.

You always slope away from me
never caught – an uncontainable ivy
wall-capped, boundary-reaching over
flow. Abundance is a killing concept
cruel to cut, necessary to survive. I can't
cut you off. I watch the weeds grow.
Turn away.

Awe

We watch the water
wonder how any one called it blue
as soon as you move it, it's clear
to those who crossed the Rubicon
Jordan Blue, Mediterranean Blue,
Tyber Blue, Danube Blue
from grey to clear, from there to here
something was unspoken.
Or was it ritually sunnier
standing stones recording shadow-long
pockets of time till the sunset bouncing
from ben to brae and back again?
Was it clear to those who built on water
walked on water, lived on water to live
that we need another word?
Blue, Blue, crossed with clouds
fisherman blue, net-driven, silver
hordes in a catch, breathless
beach-bound, boat-tilting blue.

LONGING

Paddling at the Edge

My Daddy, big and capable: invincible
always on your shoulders you carried me.
So tall, I couldn't see the top of you:
I leaned back to see you and sky

Your favourite: premature, vulnerable
I won your admiration, you love me, I know
you laughed, we danced, I sang
I want to be *Bobby's Girl*, forever

Still powerful, but smaller
still fatherly though uncertain
fiercely loyal, yet partisan, you can
infuriate me, but I love you

Love that bites back impatience
stays quiet, to make life easier.
Give, what you gave unconditionally
patiently, freely to a child.

Safe

comeliness

smoothed in roughness

a soft jaw slackened

in sleep

moon-traced

ruffled duvet

tucked in

cooried in cuddled in bedded in

car sounds

too sharp for snow

beneath the window

crackle in frost

sulphurous streetlamp winterglows

silence and engine

alternating light pattern the blind

kind

the

drawing

in

of

night.

The Presentation

Afore ye, ah dinnae dream
o' a fantoush hoose or ma' ain green:
ah hud nae money.
Afore ye, ah hud nae notion
o' a great muckle pram or fancy cot:
ah dinnae hae you tae pit in thaim.
Ah niver buskit yir room (sure, ah only hud ma' ane)
nae babbie-cloots or braw shawls
ah dinnae hae ony money!
So, ah kept ye tae masel'
afore onyone saw ye, ah kent ye
felt ye turn, helpt ye grow
felt ye kickin', kept ye tae masel'
in peace an' quiet
feet up, tea in haun, nae plans
fur the morra', jist you an' me thigither
knowin' each other.

So cuddle in an' coorie in
an' snuggle in wi'me.
Yir here noo, shoosh noo,
a wheen o' folk to see.
Nae langer jist wi' me, ma' son,
nae langer jist wae me.

Famine Village, Achill Island

Slievemore black, black against the sky
swallowing light

scattered on the mountainside my
children scramble goats among sheep

unmortared stones pile gable ends
cottages along a mossy track

plainstone hearths and shelving empty
unwelcome at the door, this gorta mor

brings no birthing on the kitchen table,
sings no dancing on the hard earth floor

in Westernmost graveyard, Mulligans
cling to the hill: now I know

how deep a hungered migration
pierces at the heart's core.

The Hunger

pinpoints of pain pummel the ribs
deep inside the cage
gnawing reality
walking never fixes
feel my baby turning

the wind turns the soil
potatoes crumble like air
disease exposed
a generation ill-formed
carrying their seed

I pass on.

Playing with Alba

she gathers, gathers – leaves, stones, sticks
makes me carry little ones
she has the big

invites me for tea
in her little house
under the chute

I wait on the swing
till she's ready
shouts me in

she shows me how she made a fire
rubs two sticks together, sighs deeply
a few times, then blows

we catch the leaves as plates
replace sand & grit & empty orange peel
topped with twigs

and we eat
in her little house
under the chute

Observance

I place my notebook on the altar rail
kneel to watch my son
water turf
cathedraled from B&Q
in the apse of his garden
forcing the fence
[a latticed rood]
push the page up to me
and I down to it
in exquisite balance.

My husband, omnipotent at the tap
controls the flow, and I
the pivotal point of the pen
distribute ink
in delicate
even
deliverance.

As I Have Loved You

you are the vine: intoxicate me
cleanse me phonetically

to cut myself is to see you bleed
to breathe in deep is to watch you exhale

would you breathe for me? I think you would breathe for me:
you could be the lung of the world

you could be the salt of my earth
the Solomon in my song
the tune to my word

a man never hates his own body: I am yours
my feet rest in your house: wash me

to love me is to love yourself
to love you is to love myself

free me : *in carcare*
between
light
&
breath
claim me to give myself in your place.

DREAMING

Penelope

My hands are heavy with waiting
My boys, too proud of you to be told
Missing is a possibility
Dreeping off walls in shows of strength
To be like Daddy, one given
A prize for perfect goodness, one
Writing, writing all the way to school
On the tram not living in the real world,
War world, our world
My heart is heavy with breaking

My attic room, full of strangers
Too many to feed without suspicion but
The butcher helps, I have to trust him
They sing slow in whispers
Complain like mice, invite danger
I cannot run away from, store trouble
I cannot eat, make loving an empty promise
I cannot help, except to expect detection
Freewheeling past every corner
On my bicycle, bell ringing, basket full.

Master Builder

My last full glance of Georgian Inverary
austere, whitewashed, imposed.
Given notice to go, but not quite ready
on the single-track bridge, I can wait.

Where the tide flows into Loch Shira
I stand, uprooted, after four generations,
my cottage workshop demolished
no more production of fine sons.

Uniformed garrison town,
I want no part of you
you want no part of me, spoiling
the view from your castle.

I bury my hearth in your Fyne Bridge wall
use my craftsmanship to give
something for seeking generations
to place me here, my ancestral home.

Lady Artist at Lascaux

A herbivore in between hunting,
I choose gathering: minerals
deep earth colour, rusty brown, burnt ochre
scoured orange, to turn a turquoise yellow.
Charcoal-heaved from fire
animals dead,

skinned, yet finely observed
teeth, bones, sinewed skulls.
Supine, sagittal planed
I imagine the way they moved
from flight to conquest, as he told me.
I draw, make my mark,

outline sometimes the stars
to give their spirits back.
These creatures of our meals
dye reluctant, curled in colour,
speak to me. They tell me:
mark again.

Annis:

It fell tae me, it wis ma turn tae leuk ower her.
Ah swear tae God, ah jist taen ma 'een fae his sister,
anely wanst, jist fir a muckle wee bit.
Her wee boukit, fair roastit, her screyms sair haunt me,
an ah hidit, shankless, couldnae shift masel':
ill-answerin Odelyn's cry- tae ma schame, ma leddy, forgie!
Ah'm sair vext, ah gied ye ma hecht, wantit tae keep ye sauf.
Ah beseek Buccmaster, dinnae fash yirsel' gangin' awa aff,
thirs skran a-plenty, lat be. But naw, he uptails.

The wan body he'd harkit tae, his grandfaither
niver keept his haunds aff me, caupit, daeless, eildit ootgaun maister.
Tha' auld wirry boggle, ill-like his ain son,
tae avenge hisel' telt the lad cracks aboot weir-like pagans,
nawt aboot the Awmichtie! Mak'd him baundless, mass, crouse;
ill-set, aye, he gang hatit his faither tae, fu' o laith.
Buccmaster fair uggit aifter his faither's lickin:
gang saft in the heid, fair wastit, he gied Odelyn a wheen o' licks tae.

Puir sowel, muckle a' feart, mairiage misbegowk,
aways telt tae haud her wheesht-
ah hud tae bide ma time, jist couldnae skyce, awa aff, as ah wantit.
She wis cannie, she wis cliver- ashuirit Buccmaster he wis boss-
but bide a wee!
Her sons, mither-sons, hart hale, hecklin' their faither, quaistenin.
Claymore girthie, gods brak, quate. Failyie.

Ah spake in gnappin earnest, tack tent.
Me n' Odelyn, we flauchtit, we laucht,
Ah luv'd her, lik ma ain, till she wis past mendin'.
Win frae, win oot, ah says, wae me, yir sons!
But naw. She wis daen.
She wis attakit, gied a dinger, dusht.
Great-hearted, maikless,
braw, snithfest,
ma bonnie Leddy,
Odelyn.

St. Patrick's Scribe

This cell is weary of me.
the story, familiar to me now:
candles burning down to wicks
tapered like the day, too dull for accuracy.
He ordained me, gave me life,
my name: Broccan Cloen; converted, tonsured, cowled:
I learned to be learned, translating Irish gaelic to Latin
mixing inks, slipping fantastic beasts in the margin.
Now, Bishops talk against him, say
it is not for the Glory of God, but his own notoriety...
Be accurate, I'm told, be bold, complete this justification,
Tell them: 'I am nothing
                    it is not for me
                    I am nothing...'
Humans no longer bartered for a loaf of bread
or children sold for wine skins, as he said
piracy scuttled with the snakes:
banished, in truth, the rule of the sword
freedom paid by the blood of Our Lord.
'I did not ask for the See of Armagh, Broccan,' he says,
'Broccan, my friend, enlighten them, illuminate,
in lux perpetua, no more darkness, tell them, we live in light!'

The day is over, capitals outlined in silver, finished in gold
my hands are inky, mottled, sore: it is done.
I carry to his cell an old man who can no longer lift a pen
or a finger, in his own defence, this gentle saint
who fought for me, paid for me, brought me out of slavery.

Solatium

She plays the glass harmonica in Central Station
on the way to a wedding, hopeful as a beggar
stealing harmony from humiliation

Something jars in mirrored rings of new blown glass
distorting madness, just behind the beat
echoes in a distant head

Put your hands on me
Moisten those fingers
Soak up the lead
I will teach you crazy

In Central Library
you bang those keys as if demented
as if what you write is important,
must be written, though I've seen your type before
and rather it would be hidden

Paedophile, Paedophile, he said
If I believed him

On the brink of brittle motherhood, sarcazo,
tearing flesh, fragments of angel chime wound with intent
putting me on edge.
We forgot to invite ourselves.

ESCAPE

Resurface

Start with escape
a release, somewhere to go.
Just go.

Empty on a journey fills up.
Empty on a journey notices you need to be filled.
Empty on a journey knows emptiness – decides to change it for something else.

Maybe barters a train for a bus.
Or a coach for a sleeper.
Or a rail for a road.

Or the moon instead.
Or the sun.
Or windscreen wipes the rain.
Or maybe not.

Maybe a backseat buys you time to adjust.
Whatever.

The emptiness becomes a filling for the journey.
Or the journey fills the empty: becomes transported.

Either way you are subject to time
fast or slow
speed variable
a particle wave
not responsible
not staying still.

Just going.
Getting out from under.

Memo

Remember: on a rainy day
          clouds low
   water pouring empty light
        remember:
how we pierced the raincloud,
              gliding in blue sky
on top of one cloud
     &   underneath another.

Nonsensical people stay on the ground
       don't walk upside down
           cloud-skimming:
stay-cation grey   sky-hemmed,
              sky-scraped.

Our rainbow-rimmed fingers
        hold the horizon: this luminous life
this luminous life   smoothed over
        the vault of the sky
    clearly   invisible
          still there*: claro*

Javito

Cowl-born, suckling
white-wrapped, launched
from dormouse to unstrung colt

smiling sometimes
your little head
couries in below my neck

a baby space I always knew
was there but forgot
till you reminded me

your little heart
lub-dub, lub-dub
on top of mine

back-patted to the rhythm we make
you show me who you are
a person who came prepared

you are beautiful.

CSI Madrid

'Let there be a landscape of open eyes
and bitter wounds on fire.
No one is sleeping in this world
I have said it before.'

Frederico Garcia Lorca, 'City Does Not Sleep'

No one is to remember who did the killing,
where the bodies are buried; lining tunnels, propping up motorways,
trundled over on the bus to Moncloa. On the Casa de Campo,
bleached bones overripe for investigation cry out.
Figure out who did it, except, there is no figuring,
the law is to forget. Everything here is about death.
On the Gran Via, we sit in a roadside café, watch film set traffic;
red carpet rolled, Star Wars ready, Storm Troopers take their revenge:
we absorb disturbance in the universe.
A pedestrian cuts like a racing car under the Matisse sky, jaywalking
straight lines, slicing bends. He has to be legislated against; so much anarchy
is dangerous to oncoming vehicles. Truth is always
ahead of the curve, paying attention to the appropriate:
hoping to be caught, but not too soon.

Villanueva de la Cañada

I went on living when you were dying
Clicked bones and guns into place
We were instructed to ignore it, even though death rattled so
Every one hundred paces four men dead,
It had to be ordinary, leaving you
You were the only one truly present
The plain of Madrid, a bourgeois coffin, open to the heat and dust.

Following the line of Mosquito Ridge, clear and lit by moonlight
Every blade of grass standing to attention, we release this village
From nationalists brave enough to use civilians as human shields
And convents, devoid of nuns become their ornate jails.

Storks swoop over the church, build their nests in the belltower
Black tipped wings spread in supplication, ring out the siesta:
We put down our guns between two and four
Report anarchist conversation in Republican bars
Find our friends incarcerated, ourselves suspect.

They tell me, 'Your family are those who fight for liberty.'
What do they know of the folk in Bellshill?
I went on living when you were dying
It had to be ordinary, leaving you.

Last Supper in Brunete

Images of the crucifixion project onto the belltower
Stations of the cross stage the Passion
betrayer's kiss as the sky darkens

she howls and rocks her son on the steps
cries and cries to the torchlit sky
senseless bloodshed senseless cruelty

politicians scuttle in the background
move undercover of darkness
wash their hands in broken dreams
hang themselves
for thirty pieces of silver

she howls at the moon
put your hands in the bullet holes
feel my wounds.

Picasso's Tears

they seep
war-torn page-torn
care-worn
stain
ghost-stretched fine-line hankies
black ink deep
etched to catch
head-tilting half-cup full
eyes
wrung wet dripping sleep-stung
a
sharp-tongued-jagged
silent screech

spacious head-room dream & dreamt wrongly
monstrous mechanics turn machines to overflow
tear monsters
caught screaming
unstoppable unbearable
grief

Over the Bay of Biscay

Sprung out from the middle as if the plane we were on was the middle
and the plane we were on was the plane itself and we were the middle
from us purple and vermillion flattened, drawn out flat on a drawing board
turquoise over the edge and navy blue on one side and the side was us
we were rimmed in orange, orange-rimmed on the rim of a rim
of a wheel, a circular window, grey-interrupted, one-sided interruption
shot from below a tinge of green from turquoise which came from navy
not red, yet red, yet only red so red it was black, squashed
into the horizon, event horizon, we were pulled
black and red and orange-planed, planed and fanned and we were burnt
red-orange-black concentrated, distilled, we were the centre
tip-wing tinged above upside down mountains dropping rain
rain below we couldn't see but had seen before in grey and black
pierce and piercing we did pierce shuddering to the upside
falling centre above the rain but not really passing blue and violet and green
in a shaft, in a pile, in a pecking order all at once and the same time
cloud-centered above the cloud in a red ball rising blue and turquoise
always always not coming down till the green was red and the blue was black
in straight lines in a plane all around us looking. It was colour we were
many faded into and beyond curved and straight, disappearing an escape
arrival a destination red-sentenced with no words yellow and green
and blue on the wing separated together at the centre of the middle
of the plane, white-orange and the plane we were on was the middle
sun-centered, rain-drowned, wing-tipped and drowning, fading and shining
weightless and held colour-centric, faded, setting yellow and burnished.
Gliding not moving in the middle not wanting, drifting but not always
surrounded, ochre-polished, separated but in always, brightened, whole.

JUDGEMENT

The Way of the Cross

The pen is polite in politics:
Marking only an 'X'
A civilised way of signing
The Cross of Saint Andrew in a box
No longer a crucifixion
To get a point across.

The aftermath is brutal in politics
Marked and sealed with a cross
Calculated, found wanting
This martyred St Andrew in a box
Ordains a Scottish crucifixion
The emphasis of loss.

So

Brexit, Brexit, a shameless exit, a British fear
a 'get me out of here, we're not winning'
no longer the boss, at a loss – this British Bulldog
running off the leash, fit to be tied, foaming
at the mouth madness, got to get away.

In Villanueva de Cañada we're welcome,
British shops, goods, food, people, business
even here, where Scots fought on the wrong side
in a war, it turns out, they were not wanted
against Franco and fascism. Altruism
died on the road, driving ambulances,
to Escorial: Julian Bell, ferrying wounded,
Gerda Taro targeted, killed on the road,
even here, we're welcome.

French Lycees, German Schules, British Colleges,
there is no separation – children taught
English for Oxford entrance exams
by Scots, English, Welsh, Irish EU citizens
with full rights and health care, families
homes, children, where do they go, from here?

Everything was fusion
Everything was whole
Everything was seamless
Everything was easy

English stubbornness, divide
where they can't conquer
separate what they can't rule

we're the immigrants here
can't you see,
we're the immigrants here
welcomed, protected
we're the immigrants here

What have you done
Brexit, in my name,
naming nameless fear
a shaming isolation
no longer living
here.

Good Morning Britain

Watching telly, toast & tea in hand
live from Buckingham Palace,
chandeliers glistening crystal shadows on sycophantic faces
(where are Del Boy & Rodney when you need them?)
the presenter breathes, 'How did they clean them?'
The expert delights in imparting her knowledge:
'In eighteenth and nineteenth century, no electricity...so many candles
hundreds of them, leaving markers of soot, staining the glass...'
A breathless repetition, 'So...how did they clean them?
'Stale bread', she says, 'Stale bread!'- her emphatic smile widens
toasting servant ingenuity when removing Victorian excess.

And they crawled for miles to find food
looked for their names on non-existent lists
built roads that went nowhere
Skibbereen, Cork, Kerry
for nineteenth century non-existent bread
children weak and diseased, population fled
Skibbereen, Cork, Kerry

Stale bread stain removers.
British ingenuity.
Sticks in my throat.

Display

"Ah've loast ma virgini'y!"
she cried at the height
of the wails and bangs
as, *contra mundum*
we stand, watching

at Paisley Abbey, the
light and fire, the falling
globes all around us
burst us into one.

And I thought, "How strange"
that she should use
this singular term of ejaculation
for ethereal ecstasy, en masse.

In the light of fading fireworks
the Abbey shrugs against the cold,
nudges us home
back to individuality.

Paisley

Paisley descends into hardened faces,
heart-burned stomach-ulcered lived-in faces
line-puckered cigarette traces blowing in & out.
Miroculous, miraculous, avuncular Paisley
junkyard Paisley, dismantled mills
pills on every corner, years without work
die-hard Paisley, don't give a fuck Paisley
dream-disabled determined Paisley
clinging on for good or ill, open spaces
lost places, bi-passed on the Foxbar bus
chopped up Paisley, bus-passed Paisley
Arnotts closed & High Street shut.

Coffee-shopped Paisley, student Paisley
Poet-lined book-shopped Radical Paisley
Tannahill-leaving grief-stricken Paisley
woven-in Paisley, heart & lung.
Song-written hard-bitten bar-studded Paisley
collar high, juke-boxed never shutting down.
Silver Thread & silver-tongued jaw-dropping Paisley
shawl-patterned Paisley, Silk Street wound.
Wallace taught & grammar'd Abbey-centric Paisley
Cradle of the Stuarts, lost and found.
Romantic, pedantic, witch-startled Paisley
martyred Paisley, hallowed ground.

You're the One That I Want

'Men are rats, listen to me, they're fleas on rats, amoebas on fleas on rats...'
Frenchy, Grease

The most buttoned up nun I ever knew didn't even tilt her head,
didn't even snore on the bus to Lourdes, there and back
pristine habit, manners unimpeachable, too sweet to be wholesome
too pure to be pink, she was shining, scrubbed clean
enough to put you off a vocation for life.
Lecturing us in sixth year, on that dangerous Olivia / Sandy moment:
when all we wanted was our moment,
many of us had it, indeed we were blessed
pressed against the hairdresser's window next to the Kelburne cinema,
four deep to see Grease. Multiple times, till the window gave in: cracked
cracked: that's what she was.
'Don't give in' she said, 'Resist- girls, let him change for you!'
'But he did change, Sister', we said: 'He changed for her...for love.'
She sighed and looked away, doe eyes rolled to heaven.

Years and three children later, surrounded by frazzled women
in replica M&S dress at their centenary Mass
three nuns got up to sing the psalm
old habits gone, one better dressed than the other
hair coiffed and makeup on, she among them
singing in harmony:
Oooh, Oooh, Oooh honey.

[*'too pure to be pink'* – Rizzo about Sandy]

LOSS

My Dad's Handwriting

Tall like the mast of a ship, crossed once, impervious:
a crow's nest of words, row upon row,
standing sail-less, a shipyard content.
Riveted in words, thrown and caught, moulted
bolted to the side of the ship, visored-on
each measured, weighted, found to be correct.

He wrote the way his father worked:
precise, ordered, to the point – a Riveter
soldering ships, choking in dry dock;
a man's shock of white hair and longshanks
silver-stomached, Clydeside blacklisted,
James Watt Quay, war-work, hard won pay.

Chippy, bitty, on the move, tales
tall as liners slip across the page
no money for dinner, pleasantly fu', my father
stole the trout from the fishmonger's window
my mother hit him with it
made him take it back
a rush of scrawl not easily deciphered
full steam, riveting in real time, drawing

a draughtsman's hand, an engineer,
painting a picture I'll never hear
Dark Loch na' Gar, whiskey chaser, bottle of beer
finish the bastard off,
abrupt the writing stops, riveting still.

Your Version

Jumped up nyaff, you know nothing
of my father, with your disdainful talk:
peripheral vascular disease
a lifetime product of smoking
directed at the computer screen
even though you know he is almost deaf,
refuse to face him, man to man.
You know nothing of the boy
who was sent to Egypt on National Service
clutching a tin of cigarettes issued by the government:
his first John Player inhaled on the way over
with fear, homesickness and a lifetime addiction,
his hearing shot from the rattle of the guns.
What do you know? Piddling, meddling podiatrist
telling Dad there is no fix – he is to blame, *smoking – you see?*
Pointing out the black bits, foot and lung, what's to be done
that humiliation won't cure, certainly make worse.
And with your history, Tommy… aneurysm,
too dangerous to operate… never heal,
wounds suppurate… what do you expect?
What do you know, of my father? What do you know?
Twenty years of not smoking, given up after my mother's cancer,
his heart attack, so strong it would have killed a lesser man,
caring for us, working, guiding, loving, providing
strength and advice. A bear of a man, always on hand, wit and music.
Newmarket pennies to place our bets, lifting us
with one hand in feats of strength.
Show him anything
discuss everything
around our table: Communism, Catholicism,
his daily communicant father
blacklisted on the Red Clyde.

What do you know, little man, of what he can handle?
How much we need him to go on, to continue
to protect him now, fierce, as he did us.
After your consultation, he clutches the wall, doesn't want to go on.
How dare you judge.
How dare you, little man.

Escape from a Deathstar

Sprung from Ward 11A at 8 o'clock
we race along the road, glimpsed:
the imprisoned view, window-captured
Dad will never escape.
                                        We plan ours,
running down the corridor, racing the lifts
bold in our dismissal. We ignore
                                        the unjust criticism of the sun
pulsating its sinking orb, rotating towards the horizon.
An upshaft of light silks the cloud,
                                        as we climb the braes
                                        wait for sundown,
rage, rage against the dying
turn to the carpark in the sky
                                       it will not stop
                                         it will not stop

the dying
sun in flight
                from the Cobbler to Ben Lomond,
                road rage against the dying
                rage race against the dying

of the light.

Haiku for Dad

(i)
Standing in your room
Many empty cabinets
Double bed stripped bare

(ii)
My Dad's wedding ring
When given to my brother
Brings sorrowful tears

(iii)
He gave my mother
Yellow roses. I place them
At their graveside now

(iv)
If you only knew
How very much I miss you
Long to hold your hand

(v)
How I so regret
Deleted phone messages
Long to hear your voice

(vi)
Talk to me in dreams
A quiet conversation
Keep me safe from harm

(vii)
How he always said
A poem was not a poem
If it did not rhyme

(viii)
In Dad's living room
Our Lady from the trenches
A statue carved, carried